Meeting Melanchthon

Meeting Melanchthon

A Brief Biographical Sketch of Philip Melanchthon and a Few Samples of His Writing

By Scott Keith

An imprint of 1517 the Legacy Project

Meeting Melanchthon: A Brief Biographical Sketch of Philip Melanchthon and a Few Samples of His Writing

© 2017 Scott Keith

All rights reserved. No part of this publication may be reproduced, distributed, or transmitted in any form or by any means, including photocopying, recording, or other electronic or mechanical methods, without the prior written permission of the publisher, except in the case of brief quotations embodied in critical reviews and certain other noncommercial uses permitted by copyright law. For permission requests, write to the publisher at the address below.

Published by:
NRP Books
PO Box 54032
Irvine, CA 92619-4032

Publisher's Cataloging-In-Publication Data
(Prepared by The Donohue Group, Inc.)
Names: Keith, Scott Leonard. | container of (work): Melanchthon, Philipp, 1497–1560. Loci communes rerum theologicarum. Selections. English.
Title: Meeting Melanchthon : a brief biographical sketch of Philip Melanchthon and a few samples of his writing / by Scott Keith.
Description: Irvine, CA : NRP Books, an imprint of 1517 the Legacy Project, [2017] | Summary: A compilation of blog posts from 1517Legacy.com, with a brief introduction to the life of Philip Melanchthon and selected translations of a few of his works. | Includes bibliographical references and index.
Identifiers: ISBN 978-1-945978-70-8 (softcover) | ISBN 1-945978-70-8 (softcover) | ISBN 978-1-945978-71-5 (ebook) | ISBN 1-945978-71-6 (ebook)
Subjects: LCSH: Melanchthon, Philipp, 1497–1560. | Theology–History–16th century.
Classification: LCC PA8550.Z5 K45 2017 (print) | LCC PA8550.Z5 (ebook) | DDC 274.009–dc23

NRP Books, an imprint of 1517. The Legacy Project, is committed to packaging and promoting the finest content for fueling a new Lutheran Reformation. We promote the defense of the Christian faith, confessional Lutheran theology, vocation and civil courage.

Cover design by Peter Voth.

Printed in the United States of America

Contents

Meeting Melanchthon: An Introduction. 1

The Early Years 7

Melanchthon's Magnum Opus 13

Work, Work, Work. 21

The Birthday of the Lutheran Church 27

Freewheeling Libertine or Law Dog?. 33

A Man of Trouble 39

The Conclusion. 45

The Method of the
"Loci Communes"—1526 51

The Uses of the Divine Law. 59

Concerning the Gospel 65

Justification and Faith 73

Notes 81

Meeting Melanchthon

An Introduction

Earlier this month, I taught a class on Philip Melanchthon at St. John's Lutheran Church in Frasier, Michigan. At the end of class, I was asked if I would recommend a short biography on Melanchthon suitable for a layperson. Sadly, I said no. Most of the short biographies are out of print and very expensive, and most of the modern works are written for academic audiences. So I decided to do a short series as a brief introduction to the life and times of Philip Melanchthon. As we continue to celebrate the five hundredth anniversary of the Reformation this year, I think that this booklet, which appeared previously as a series of blog posts on 1517Legacy.com, will be helpful and pair nicely with the two *Thinking Fellows* podcasts on Melanchthon.

Now most scholars consider Melanchthon to be a Reformation enigma. He, the developer of the Reformation doctrine of forensic justification, is contrarily condemned as a synergist. Known well as the Protestant preceptor of Germany, he was Martin Luther's lifelong friend, colleague, teacher of Greek, and fellow reformer. Upon arriving at Wittenberg, Melanchthon was a theologian neither by trade nor by training. He was a classically trained expert in classical languages, neo-Latin poet, textbook author, Greek scholar, humanist, and above all, an educator.

Melanchthon's lectures at the University of Wittenberg would commonly draw upward of four hundred students. Along with his work in the development of the German public education system and the reform of the German universities, this earned him the title of the Protestant preceptor of Germany. In both form and function, he was a theologian and a reformer.

Melanchthon was a chief formative influence on the development of historical Protestantism as the author of the first Protestant systematic theology and author of the principal Protestant confession of faith. His *Loci Communes Theologici* (*Common Topics of Theology*) was used as a textbook for pastors and teachers of the Lutheran faith for more than a hundred years, and through the *Augsburg Confession*, nearly all Protestant denominations have been influenced.

Philip Melanchthon was a humanist, an expert in classical languages and literature, and from an early age, he excelled in Hebrew, Greek, Latin, rhetoric, dialectic, and philosophy. He was the eldest son of George, a respected and somewhat famous metalsmith and maker of suits of armor, and Barbara, daughter of a prosperous merchant. Born Philip Schwarzerdt, his name was changed to Melanchthon by his great-uncle Reuchlin, the famous humanist, lawyer, and Hebrew scholar. This was done after the death of Melanchthon's father and was meant as a compliment to the promising young pupil. He received his bachelor of liberal arts from the University of Heidelberg on June 11, 1511, and his master of arts degree from the University of Tübingen on January 25, 1514. With the degrees came the right to teach and lecture on the classics.

Melanchthon was called as professor of the Greek language to Wittenberg University on August 26, 1518, while still only twenty-one years of age. Greek and the study of languages were Melanchthon's first loves and true passions, followed closely by rhetoric, dialectic, and philosophy. His passion for these disciplines led to early recognition. Melanchthon was already a well-known humanist leader and teacher of rhetoric and dialectic when he arrived at Wittenberg. By 1517, Melanchthon had already grabbed the attention of the famous humanist Erasmus of Rotterdam, who wrote in a letter to one of his friends, "I think highly of Melanchthon and place great hope in him. May Christ preserve this youth among us with long life!"

It was in Wittenberg that Melanchthon met Dr. Martin Luther. Together, the two began their lifelong journey of reform together. Not long after his arrival in Wittenberg, Melanchthon began to teach Luther Greek. This instruction was to have far-reaching results, for it brought Luther clarity concerning the faith. He wrote in 1519, "But more recently I have followed Philip Melanchthon as my teacher in Greek. He is a young man in respect to his body, but a hoary-headed old sage regarding his intellectual powers."

Though he was offered a doctorate on several occasions, he was not a doctor of theology. His learning and intelligence were such that Luther once remarked after the Leipzig debate of 1519, "This one man's opinion and authority mean more to me than many thousand miserable Ecks. I would not hesitate to yield my authority to this ingenious grammarian if he should disagree with me, even though I am Master of Arts, philosophy, and theology and adorned with nearly all Eck's titles."

The Early Years

Early Life and Education

Philip (also spelled Philipp) was born to George and Barbara Schwarzerdt in Bretten in 1497. Philip had four siblings: Anna (1499), Georg (1500 or 1501), Margarete (1506), and Barbara (1508). All were born in his grandparents' house in the electoral Saxon residential town of Bretten. Melanchthon's father, Georg Schwarzerdt, born in Heidelberg, was a master of gunnery founding and was skilled in forging lightweight, durable armor. Because of his skills, Georg was elevated to the office of electoral master armorer and thus needed to remain in Heidelberg. Melanchthon's mother, Barbara, came from the wealthy merchant family of Reuter.

Melanchthon's grandfather was the one who ensured a thorough early education in Latin for Philip and his brother, Georg, as well as for two grandsons of the Reuter family, by hiring well-known Johannes Unger from Pforzheim as the boys' tutor. The death of Melanchthon's father and grandfather in 1508 ended the childhood of eleven-year-old Philip. From this point on, his education and contribution to the burgeoning humanist movement of his day would be his vocation.

Johannes Reuchlin, a famous humanist and Hebrew scholar, was Philip's great-uncle and took some responsibility for Philip's university education. Upon learning of Philip's ability in Greek, and following the humanist tradition of his day, Reuchlin gave him the Greek name "Melanchthon." In March of 1509, Reuchlin exclaimed, "Your name is Schwarzerdt (German for 'black earth') you are a Greek, and so your new name shall be Greek. Thus, I will call you Melanchthon which means black earth."

University Education

In 1509, Philip entered the University of Heidelberg with the intention of earning his bachelor of arts (BA) degree. At Heidelberg he studied philosophy, rhetoric, astronomy/astrology, Latin, and Greek. He earned his BA in 1512 at the age of fifteen. He had wanted to enter the master of arts (MA) program at Heidelberg, but his entrance into that program was barred by the faculty, who claimed he was too young to pursue the degree. It is more likely that his high intelligence and ability at such a young age were intimidating to well-ensconced faculty.

Upon Reuchlin's advice, Philip instead entered the MA program at the University of Tübingen. At Tübingen he studied philosophy, Latin, Greek, classical literature, law, medicine, and mathematics. He graduated with his MA degree in 1516 at the age of nineteen. He almost immediately published a Greek grammar that was widely used in the initial instruction of Greek for many years.

At Wittenberg

During the 1518–19 academic year, Philip joined the faculty at the University of Wittenberg. He was called to Wittenberg to be a professor of Greek. He had wanted to teach theology as well, but he was not qualified. It is worthy to note that Philip was essentially a philologist and classicist by training, not a theologian. As a workaround, Philip was pleased to teach his students Greek by teaching them to read John's Gospel.

He continued his studies at Wittenberg with Luther as well as on his own. At Wittenberg he mastered Hebrew by studying with Luther and theology by means of more intense study with Luther and in-depth exegesis of the Gospel of John and Paul's Epistle to the church at Rome. Philip still desired to teach theology but needed a qualification to do so. Thus, in 1519, he completed his theological treatise (thesis) granting him a degree in theology and affording him a second appointment (professor of Greek and theology). Within his baccalaureate theses, the term "imputation" is first used to describe how Christ's righteousness is imparted to the believer: "All righteousness is a gracious imputation of Christ."

Family Life and Friendship with Luther

Initially, Luther was not drawn to Philip as a friend, as he looked sickly and weak to Luther.

Soon, they became good friends and partners. Luther encouraged him to get married because he feared for his health and well-being. In 1521, Philip married Katherine Krapp, daughter of the mayor of Wittenberg. Together they had four children: Anna (1522), Philipp (1525), Georg (1527), and Magdalena (1533). Even though Luther and Philip learned to be good friends, their wives never did. It was reported by several of their Wittenberg colleagues that the two ladies would often refuse to be in the same room with one another.

Luther's influence on the young Philip was great, and the reverse was true as well. Philip influenced Luther with the humanist principles of *ad fontes* (a return to the sources), his knowledge of Greek, and his diverse classical learning. In 1519, Luther said, "But more recently I have followed Philip Melanchthon as my teacher in Greek. He is a young man in respect to his body, but a hoary-headed old sage in regard to his intellectual powers." Luther influenced Philip in the areas of theology—especially law and gospel and the theology of the cross versus the theology of glory—and finding real comfort in the proclamation of the gospel.

The two men, early colleagues and reluctant friends, would become a nearly unstoppable theological team during the Reformation.

Melanchthon's Magnum Opus

Luther under the Ban, Melanchthon Hard at Work

In 1521—the same year Melanchthon married his wife—at the Diet of Worms, Martin Luther was convicted of heresy and placed under a papal bull and an imperial ban. The ban meant that he was an outlaw and could be killed or imprisoned on sight. It was only the grace and quick thinking of his elector, Fredrick the Wise, that saved Luther's bacon. Elector Fredrick whisked Luther off to the Wartburg castle for safekeeping. Yet while Dr. Luther was contending with the papal bull against him, confessing the Christian faith at Worms, and writing sermons for preaching in the Castle Church and elsewhere, Melanchthon was at work developing the first Lutheran "system" of theology. This work was destined to exert a powerful influence on the Lutheran Reformation and marks an epoch in the history of Christian theology. The work in question was entitled the *Loci Communes Theologici*, or *Common Topics of Theology*.

Early Editions

The work was originally written during the tumultuous early 1520s (the first official edition was published in 1521) in Wittenberg as the enthusiasts were taking advantage of Luther's exile to the Wartburg castle to cause utter chaos among the people. Melanchthon's claim was that his desire in writing this work was to "make all Christians thoroughly conversant with the Holy Scripture alone." This work on which Melanchthon was laboring utilized an age-old method of arranging categories of thought topically into loci, or topics of theology. Melanchthon, as several theologians who predated him had done, arranged theological topics as drawn from the Holy Scriptures—specifically from Paul's Epistle to the Romans—topically.

In 1521, after sending it to Luther for revisions, he published the first version of the *Loci Communes Theologici*. By the end of the year 1525, he had published eighteen Latin editions in addition to various printings of a German translation done by his colleague Spalatin. This early work was characterized by a blanket rejection of all philosophy, particularly any form of Aristotelian philosophy. Luther claimed that this edition of the *Loci* should be added to the Christian canon. This edition is uniquely (synthetically) arranged—that is, it is arranged beginning from matters of salvation, to the means of grace, with God as the author of salvation.

Middle Editions

In the period encompassing 1533(5)–41, or the middle editions, Melanchthon greatly expanded the *Loci* and changed the style of arrangement from soteriological to synthetic or creedal. In 1535 came the great controversy over supposed synergism within the doctrine of justification in the *Loci*. It is said that within the 1535 *Loci*, Melanchthon states that "good works are necessary to salvation" in seeming opposition to the hard Pauline stance taken in the 1521 edition. Also, it is in this edition of the *Loci* that the problematic formulation of three "causes" in conversion emerges as consisting of the preaching of the word, the work of the Holy Spirit, and the human will, which then does not refuse the Holy Spirit's work. Though Luther did not publicly oppose this edition of the *Loci*, it is viewed as Melanchthon's first steps toward serious doctrinal error.

Later Editions

The later editions were published from 1543 to 1559, with the final edition being published just one year before Melanchthon's death in 1560. This period marks even greater expansion of the *Loci*; this edition is four times the size of the original 1521 edition. Gone are the statements dealt with in this study, "that good works are necessary to salvation," but still included is the controversial formulation on three causes of conversion. Also, this period marks greater reliance on classical sources like Cicero, Aristotle, and Homer. During this period, Melanchthon undertook the first German translation of the *Loci* that he would complete himself. While Luther was still alive when the 1543 editions were published, he again did not condemn Melanchthon's formulation on conversion but praised the work. As a side note, this is the edition on which Martin Chemnitz lectures and bases his *Loci Theologici*.

Why the Loci Method?

In the dedicatory epistle to the later editions of the *Loci*, Melanchthon sets out in no uncertain terms his reasons for ordering theology topically and the pedagogical necessity of passing the Christ-centered method down into posterity. According to Melanchthon, the ordering of theology in a topical and understandable way serves as a comfort to those who are in doubt: "It is useful to have true and transparent testimony of the separate articles of Christian doctrine, divided in an orderly way, just as if they had been laid out on a table, so that when our intellect is coerced to doubt or given over to threats, that we should see another way of thinking, one which will instruct those in trembling, raise, confirm, and console them." Furthermore, he quotes the psalmist in a sympathetic understanding that only the Scriptures can provide true light and consolation in matters of Christian doctrine. These exercises of faith are necessary and should not be unknown to the faithful, of which the prophet has said, "Your Word is a light to my feet."

Second Order Serving First Order

Additionally, this teaching is to be passed down generationally, from scholars who develop and challenge the propositions, to pastors who are taught by the scholars, to parishioners who hear the words of proclamation from the pastors. This is second-order topical teaching in service to first-order categorical preaching of the forgiveness of sins.

In the *Loci*, Melanchthon shows an urgency for those who are tasked, as he was, with teaching those who would be faithful pastors of God's flock, the church, to show diligence and love of scriptural truth. The gifts of second-order teaching are to be passed to the people by way of the first-order preaching by the "ministers of the Gospel." A minister is one who heals. Healing of the sinner comes by forgiveness of sins given in the proclaimed and categorical message of the gospel. Therefore, Melanchthon spent the time needed in second-order topics to teach those who will truly forgive sins in a first-order categorical way—by being ministers of the gospel of Jesus Christ.

It's All about the Gospel of Christ

What is imperative in everything that establishes Melanchthon's ordering of theological topics is a reliance on the justification of the sinner before God on account of Christ, breathed into men by means of the proclamation of Holy Scriptures, specifically the gospel of Christ.

Work, Work, Work

Early Days at Wittenberg

Contrary to popular opinion, Melanchthon never served as a parish pastor. Unlike Luther, he was not known as a preacher. But as John Schofield points out in his work *Philip Melanchthon and the English Reformation*, his 1519 bachelor of divinity degree earned at Wittenberg and his appointment to the faculty at the University of Wittenberg made him the first ordained professor of Greek in Germany.

In 1525, he and Luther received special permission to read and teach whatever they desired at the university, though Melanchthon continued to teach Greek. For Melanchthon, Greek was more than a subject to learn and teach; it was the root of learning, and he believed that a poor knowledge of Greek led to poor theology. In place of Luther, who remained under the imperial ban, Melanchthon became the spokesman of the Reformation at imperial diets, princely halls, and theological colloquies.

Beginning in 1519, Melanchthon began to develop his theology. In his baccalaureate theses, Melanchthon used the term "imputation" to describe how Christ's righteousness is imparted to the believer. Imputation is a transfer of benefit or harm from one person to another. In theology, imputation is used negatively to refer to the transfer of the sin and guilt of one man, Adam, to the rest of humankind. Positively, imputation refers to the righteousness of one man, Christ, being transferred to those who believe in him for salvation. Melanchthon says, "All righteousness is a gracious imputation of Christ."

This development shows an amazing advancement in the fight against the late medieval scholastic Roman Catholic view of infused righteousness, and in many ways, it was the heart of the Reformation. It is in the development of the doctrine of forensic justification by faith that Melanchthon made his chief contribution to the theological development of the Reformation.

Singular Focus

The proclamation of God's free grace declared to the sinner on account of the person and work of Christ Jesus was the mainstay of Melanchthon's doctrinal development. As this singular focus permeated his intellectual world, it led him to develop the Reformation message systematically. The loci, or topical method, that Melanchthon used for "doing theology" necessitated that he identify one central topic or doctrine and then build all other doctrines off of that central teaching. For Melanchthon, salvation by grace alone, through faith alone, and on account of Christ alone was the center. This is clearly seen in his *Loci Communes*, the *Augsburg Confession*, and the *Apology of the Augsburg Confession* (*Apology*).

Three Periods of Influence

Melanchthon's theological career can be segmented into three distinct periods. Period one was the early years. During this period, Melanchthon began to lecture and produced the first editions of the *Loci Communes*. Period two was the era of heavy work and theological maneuvering. This period followed the writing of the *Augsburg Confession* and the *Apology* and represented a period of intense writing and theological ambassadorship on the part of Melanchthon. Lastly, the third period was after Luther's death and was characterized by scandal and chaos both within Lutheranism in general and in Melanchthon's life and works more specifically.

A Controversial Figure

Unlike Luther, in later life, Melanchthon was less clear and lucid in his theological developments. Melanchthon's later theological developments underwent changes as he made unfortunate concessions that often cause modern theologians and historians to regard him as a betrayer, synergist, and crypto-Calvinist. In most cases, the true impact of his later theological changes is overstated. Many of the charges that have been levied against him, though in some cases true of his followers, were not necessarily true of him. Charges of synergism, crypto-Calvinism, and works righteousness would be difficult to prove from a reading of Melanchthon's own theological writings drawn from the primary sources.

Unfortunate Changes

Nonetheless, Melanchthon made several unfortunate changes to his writings that at best left followers and supporters of Luther confused and at worst left them feeling abandoned by Melanchthon. He made at least three major sets of changes to the *Loci Communes* and on multiple occasions rewrote the *Augsburg Confession*. The name of Melanchthon has often been associated with controversy and divergence from the "Lutheran norm" or "authentic Lutheranism." This is an unfortunate legacy for one of the fathers of Lutheranism, the Lutheran Confessions, and Lutheran systematic theology.

Lasting Influence

His influence spans far beyond the controversy and can be seen not only in the writings of Luther but in the later Lutheran Confessions, most notably the *Formula of Concord*, as well as in the doctrinal development of later Lutheran orthodoxy. At worst his legacy is one of a confused contemporary and progeny of Luther. At the very least, he ought to be considered an influential reformer and original rediscoverer of the doctrine of imputation and forensic justification by faith alone. As a brilliant scholar and inept leader, his work ought not be discounted due to his lack of seeming fortitude. Luther he was not, but those of us who hold historical Lutheranism to be a correct exposition of biblical doctrine owe much to this man, the quintessential bookworm of the Reformation.

The Birthday of the Lutheran Church

By Order of the Emperor

To develop a united front against the Turks, Emperor Charles V decreed that an imperial diet would convene at Augsburg to deal with the "evangelical problem," among other things. The emperor announced that the diet would convene on April 8, 1530.

Prior to the diet, the outlook for the new evangelical protestors was far from hopeful. The emperor had completed his conquest of Italy and was now positioned to deal with Luther and his ilk. He needed those protecting these protestors (Protestants) to get in line and help him fight off the Turks. The only obstacle left in front of the emperor was the unresolved issue of Germany. The religious upheaval had its run, and it was time to act. Making matters even worse, the evangelical princes appeared to be hopelessly divided.

The *Torgau Articles*

Elector John of Torgau instructed Luther and some of his colleagues, including Melanchthon, to prepare a document treating especially "those articles because which it is said division, both in faith and in outward church customs and ceremonies, continues." The group of men worked on the statement and presented it to the elector in Torgau. This document came to be known as the *Torgau Articles*. The document sent to Torgau treated the following articles of faith: Human Doctrines and Ordinances, Marriage of Priests, Both Kinds in the Mass, Confession, the Power of Bishops, Ordination, Monastic Vows, Invocation of Saints, German Singing, Faith and Works, the Office of the Keys (papacy), the Ban, Marriage, and the Private Mass.

Articles from Luther's Pen

The *Marburg Articles* were authored by Luther and were the initial Lutheran statement of faith.

Luther drew up these fifteen articles in 1529, six months prior to the Diet of Augsburg. It is somewhat commonly held that it was on these *Marburg Articles* that Melanchthon based the teachings contained in the *Augsburg Confession*. While it may be true that Melanchthon used the *Marburg Articles* as a foundational document for the *Augsburg Confession*, what he developed at Augsburg is a far more complete work and obviously bears the mark of his unique style and scholarly approach.

While at a stopover at Coburg while traveling to Augsburg, Melanchthon was commissioned to author what would be considered a vindication of why the elector of Saxony had stewarded religion in his lands. Luther, who was still considered a heretic and outlaw, could not attend the diet, though he desperately wanted to go. Luther left the diet to Melanchthon, who became Luther's chief representative there.

From Melanchthon's Pen

Melanchthon wrote the *Augsburg Confession*, though he communicated with Luther daily by letter, making sure that everything was to his liking. The Catholics had relied on Johann Eck, a famous theologian, to make their argument. He did so in something called the *Four Hundred and Four Theses*. The *Augsburg Confession* was in some ways intended to be a refutation of Eck's *Four Hundred and Four Theses*. In them, Eck found it necessary to quote out of context from Luther, Melanchthon, and other reformers such as Carlstadt and Zwingli, and he labeled them all to be heretics. What was used as the defense against Eck was Melanchthon's Protestant confession of evangelical faith, the *Augustana* (*Augsburg Confession*).

Melanchthon had assisted in the composition of both the *Schwabach* and the *Marburg Articles*. He used these prior documents and reworked the ideas therein to fit the changed situation. The time-constrained authoring of the *Augustana* caused Melanchthon great angst. Melanchthon was never satisfied with his own literary output, and the *Augsburg Confession* was no exception.

Melanchthon believed that he was compiling the true evangelical doctrine. Luther had, at least in large part, developed this new evangelical doctrine. Melanchthon valued Luther's opinion highly and sent the first draft to Luther for examination. Luther returned it to him with utterances of praise. This confession was not to be the theology of Luther or Melanchthon but of the confessing evangelicals. This theology did not belong to Luther, nor did it belong to Melanchthon; it belonged to Christ.

The Presentation

On June 15, 1530, the confession was read. As was Melanchthon's habit, the *Augsburg Confession* was improved, polished, perfected, and partly "recast" right up until the moment it was read. Even after Luther read the document, many changes were made. It would not be until June 23 that those in attendance signed the *Augsburg Confession*. On June 24, Cardinal Campeggio lobbied for complete suppression of the Protestant sects. On June 25, Christian Bayer read the *Augustana* to the emperor and a portion of the assembly a second time. What Melanchthon had prepared at Augsburg was to become the first and formative creed of the new Lutheran Church. Dr. Bayer was to have read the document so loudly that even those standing outside the hall heard him clearly, though the emperor was said to have slept through the momentous occasion.

Signatories and Heroes

In June of 1530, the princes and electors of the free Protestant states of Saxony signed the *Augustana*. The Lutheran historian F. Bente says that the signers were "Christian heroes, who were not afraid to place their names under the Confession, although they knew it might cost them goods, and blood, life and limb." Among these heroes was Elector John. Bente also notes that "when Melanchthon called the elector's attention to the possible consequences of signing the Augsburg Confession, the latter answered that he would do what was right, without concerning himself about his electoral dignity; he would confess his Lord, whose cross he prized higher than all the power of the world." The signing of the *Augsburg Confession* on June 30, 1530, is considered by many to be the birthday of the Lutheran Church.

Freewheeling Libertine or Law Dog?

We All Love a Good Controversy

The late 1520s brought controversy to the budding Lutherans and Melanchthon. Among them was what would come to be known as the Antinomian Controversy. Johan Agricola, a colleague and preacher, had begun to argue that the law no longer needed to be preached to Christians because the regenerate was free from the power of the law.

At the same time, in the late 1520s and early 1530s, Melanchthon's theology became utterly reliant on the idea that justification is a purely forensic act whereby the unjust sinner is declared just on account of Christ (*propter Christum*). For Melanchthon, the problem with this formulation occurs in that this leaves little room for good works, even of the outward or civil type.

The Law Systematized

With his humanist bent toward the need for a moral and theological reform of the church, Melanchthon could not allow this to stand. Further, his need of achieving the definitional clarity that the loci method demanded was not served by allowing this "loose end" to remain untied. Thus in the 1535 edition of the *Loci*, he developed the idea of uses—or, more properly, functions—of the law. He hoped that this formulation would put to rest the controversy over the preaching of the law and prove once and for all that Christians needed to continue to hear the law. In 1535, he tried to clarify just why that is.

So then, in the 1535 edition of the *Loci*, the definition of the law became exaggerated and expanded to include three uses, or functions, and each is given a clearly defined set of categories under which it is active.

The First Function

The first function of the law, which Melanchthon delineates, is that which Luther and all the Reformers would have used. It is the civil function of the law. Not only will this function restrain sin, but it is also known to all, regenerate and unregenerate alike. It can and will lead to a certain type of knowledge of God, a simple knowledge of His existence and a fear of Him.

According to this function of the law, God grants civil order to all people. He establishes government for the common good, and this function contains threats and promises. Melanchthon says, "And for this discipline, God has ordained (1) magistrates; (2) the law; (3) common instruction; (4) punishments; (5) human suffering. Also pertinent are sayings of Paul from Galatians 3:24: 'So then, the law was our guardian until Christ came.'" (*Note*: Melanchthon loves lists!)

Function Number Two: The Real Deal!

The second function of the law is the theological function. This is not part of the law of nature, but it is one and the same with the divine law of God. The primary function of the law is to accuse and drive the sinner to repentance and Christ. Melanchthon says, "The second function belongs to the Divine Law, and is the chief function, it shows us our sin, accuses us, petrifies us, and condemns the conscience." The chief function of the law is to condemn. As stated, the law cannot lead to salvation. So then, its primary function is to terrify the conscience of the sinner. In fact, this function of the law does even more: "This understanding in the same way teaches that the Law terrifies the conscience, because it always accuses us, and not only does it make accusations against us, but it shows us our natural weakness and condemns us of our ignorance towards God, our contempt of God, and our similar affections."

The Third Function: This One Is for You, Christians

When teaching the believer about the third function of the law, Melanchthon claims (1) the third function of the law is for those justified by faith; (2) it teaches them about good works and obedience; (3) the regenerate is free from the law according to justification; (4) according to obedience, the law remains as a rule not a hammer; (5) obedience should be begun in the regenerate so that they do at least some part of the law; (6) but this is not for salvation, for this is on account of Christ; (7) but it is for obedience since it belongs to good works. There is an ontological assumption present in Melanchthon's view and method of defining the law. It seems to be that, at least on some level or under some function, the Christian is capable of righteousness unto it. Melanchthon is sophisticated enough to try to avoid the explicit consequences of this type of thinking. Yet it is implicit and needs to be exposed whether he sees it as a necessary exposition or not. Thus in Melanchthon, though the law cannot save, the gospel correctly understood would at least lead to an outward righteousness, which can be measured by the third function of the law.

Clearly Unclear

Perhaps the problem is that Melanchthon's initial attempts at clarity left many unanswered questions. To the first question asked, "Does the third function of the law place a requirement on the regenerate to 'do something' in order to be saved?" the answer, at least from the 1535 *Loci*, is no. To the second question, "Where is the action in Melanchthon's theology? Is it the action on the part of God or on the part of the regenerate?" the answer is both, as can be seen in Melanchthon's formula. Melanchthon says, "The third function of the Law in those who are justified by faith is that which teaches them about good works, and teaches them what works are pleasing to God." Yet he expands, saying, "But now that we are justified, it is necessary to obey God."

But at Least the Crisis Was Averted . . . Right?

Not really. Melanchthon's attempt at calming the storm with this formulation eventually came to naught. As said above, he left too many questions unanswered. Antinomians still claimed that the law was not needed. Others relied too heavily on the law, teaching that it could do things Scripture denies it does. Some believed they were the users of the law rather than God. Attempts were made by later Lutherans in the *Formula of Concord* to clear things up again. The formulators of the *Formula* wonderfully stated the law's functions and its limits. But alas, even though the *Formula* had laid down the "official doctrine," the Antinomian Controversy persisted and perhaps does to this day.

A Man of Trouble

The First Missteps

Melanchthon was the consummate tinkerer and was never completely satisfied with anything he authored. Directly after the presentation of the *Augsburg Confession* and the publication of the *Apology*, Melanchthon began to make changes to the *Augsburg Confession*. These changes have become known as the *Variata*, or *Altered Augsburg Confession*. Up to 1540, these were mostly minor changes in wording. However, in 1540 and 1542, Melanchthon made changes to Article X, which caused considerable controversy. In Article X of the *Variata*, Melanchthon makes the language concerning the presence of Christ in the Lord's Supper less precise to make the article more acceptable to the Reformed. While these changes were not extreme, they should not have been made as men had laid their lives on the line for what they originally signed in 1530. To change a document men had pledged their lives, reputations, and fortunes to defend was certainly a mistake.

To Preach the Law or Not to Preach the Law

Throughout his life, Melanchthon was embroiled in quite a few internal as well as external controversies. Most of these occurred after Luther's death but some during Luther's life. Most notable among these is the so-called Antinomian Controversy with John Agricola. In 1525, unknown to him, the *Saxon Visitation Articles* that Melanchthon had written for the instruction of Lutheran pastors were published. In these Melanchthon said, "The preaching of the Law incites repentance," and "the Law must be preached to terrify." John Agricola, who sought to be a professor of theology at Wittenberg, objected, claiming, "The Law has been abolished by the Gospel and repentance must come not from knowledge of the Law, but from the Gospel." This spawned a rigorous publishing battle that lasted from 1527 to 1556.

After Luther's Death

In 1548, controversies surrounding Melanchthon's involvement in the Leipzig and Augsburg Interims began to occur. In May of 1548, the emperor and his armies defeated the coalition of evangelical princes called the Schmalkaldic League. The emperor imposed a series of religious practices on the evangelical lands that brought back many Roman Catholic (papist) practices. This "compromise" was called the Augsburg Interim.

The Augsburg Interim was no compromise at all, and this was unacceptable to Lutheran theologians. Later that year, Melanchthon assisted in the authoring of the Leipzig Interim, which he said would protect justification while compromising on things that were indifferent. Mostly, Melanchthon compromised on worship practice, allowing some of the more objectionable Roman Catholic practices to find their way back into Lutheran worship. Many of these practices have once more found their way into Lutheran worship, but that is fodder for another article.

The worship compromises of the Interims brought forth a slew of trouble for Melanchthon. The Interim Controversy lead to the Adiaphoristic Controversy (1548–55) with the Gnesio Lutherans (authentic Lutherans). His chief antagonist in this fight was Matthias Flacius. Flacius and others held it to be wrong to observe ceremonies that would normally be considered indifferent if those usually indifferent practices were imposed by force. In such cases, a false impression is created, implying that such practices are necessary even though they are not. The Gnesios confessed, "Nothing is an adiaphoron when confession and offense are involved."

The Majoristic Controversy was brought about by Professor George Major (1502–74) of the University of Wittenberg. Major taught that "good works are necessary to salvation" and that "it is impossible for a man to be saved without good works." He was attacked by several Gnesio Lutherans, especially Matthias Flacius. Melanchthon was seen to side with George Major in the Interims in the idea that good works are necessary to salvation, because in the 1535 *Loci Communes*, Melanchthon seems to claim the same.

The Synergistic Controversy (1535–60) involved Melanchthon changing ideas on the freedom of the will and the responsibility of man in conversion. In the 1535 *Loci Communes*, following Aristotle, Melanchthon wrote that there are three cooperating causes in conversion: (1) God's word, (2) the Holy Spirit, (3) and man's will, which does not resist God's word. In fact, Melanchthon taught that the will was the material cause or thing changed by the word and the Spirit, but the confusion and charge of synergism persisted.

Who Led Lutherans after Luther's Death?

The obvious answer is Philip Melanchthon. But the many controversies, his changes to the *Loci Communes* and *Augsburg Confession*, as well as his position on the Interims cast doubt on his leadership abilities. So the question became, "Are you a Gnesio or a Philipist?" A Gnesio Lutheran believed they held the upper hand, especially on the issues of the bondage of the will and things *adiaphora*. The Philipists called themselves followers of Melanchthon and believed they embodied the true spirit of the Wittenberg theology. The truth is that neither side held all the cards, as the compromises of the *Formula of Concord* would illustrate. The true question wasn't "Who followed Luther?" but instead what was scriptural and in line with the teachings of the churches of the *Augsburg Confession*. The answer given in the theology of the *Formula of Concord* is a blend of Luther, Melanchthon, and the many others who shaped the Lutheran Reformation.

The Conclusion

The Search

Thus we are at the end of our brief investigation of Philip Melanchthon—his theology, teachings, and writings (especially the *Loci Communes*) and his role as a theological ambassador, reformer, and good friend of Martin Luther. This short series has also attempted to show that many, if not all, of the attempts that have been made to reveal or identify tensions or errors in Melanchthon's theology have arisen primarily from anachronistic presuppositions of inconsistencies with Luther or are problems that have their grounding in modern systematic and dogmatic relevancies.

Hopefully, this has been a search that ends in the recovery of a Reformation figure who was dedicated to the biblical doctrine of justification by grace alone, through faith alone, as brought to the sinner by the proclamation of the gospel of Christ, and lived out in the lives of Christians everywhere.

Even so, an attempt has here been made to put forward a suitable frame of reference for accurately understanding Melanchthon's systematic concerns regarding the nature of faith, grace, and the need for good works in the Christian life. These are expressed in many of his writings such as the *Loci Communes* (in various editions), the *Augsburg Confession*, and the *Apology of the Augsburg Confession*.

Melanchthon's Theology

One of Melanchthon's theological formulations was his conclusion that good works are necessary—that they are made up of acts of love and the preaching of the gospel to souls in need and that they do not earn salvation but rather flow from it. His quest for definitional clarity was inseparably related to both his exegetical and theological tasks: a clear explanation of the text itself and the establishment of logical order as gleaned inductively from the text and revealed through the mechanism of the loci. The result is that the definitional clarity of individual words in the book of Romans, by way of the loci method, was often as determinative for Melanchthon's sense of order, as was the whole of the content or overall organization of Romans itself.

We have seen the importance of classical studies and biblical humanism on Melanchthon's thought and the trouble that he stumbled into by his sometimes overreliance on his humanist learning. Together, Melanchthon's humanism and his knowledge of the Scriptures brought him to a new understanding of the justification, faith, and necessity of good works.

An Anniversary Celebration

As we celebrate the five hundredth anniversary of the Reformation, many modern theologians seem to desire a Reformation—or at least a Lutheranism—devoid of Melanchthon and his humanism. Yet the Lutheran Reformation did not happen that way. The church of today should learn from Melanchthon how to communicate with the world of its day—not shunning its culture (as in the case of postmodernism) but rather mastering the ability to communicate to it.

An Unsteady Alliance

The alliance between humanism and Christianity, which once proved so useful, ought to be renewed today. The postmodern man is just now beginning to feel the pain of hopelessness produced by its nihilistic ideations. The spiritual void, meaninglessness, and bankruptcy of this age are evident everywhere. Once again the need for the message of righteousness on account of Christ alone needs to be shared; and it is the job, as Melanchthon correctly stated, of the Christian to do it. It is definitional to being a Christian.

The End

Born in 1497, Melanchthon died on April 19, 1560. Toward the end of his life, Melanchthon was so under attack and embroiled in controversy that he wished for death so that he could be reunited with his beloved wife, who had died some years before. When he was dying, he turned to his son-in-law, a doctor, and prayed, "Lord save me from the ravings of the theologians."

In glory, those worries are now far behind Melanchthon. Praise be to God.

In retracing Melanchthon's steps—humanist, philologist and theologian—we have perhaps revealed the path by which people of our time might find hope and meaning in the life to come and this life as well.

The Method of the "Loci Communes"—1526

By Philip Melanchthon,
Translated by Scott L. Keith,
PhD; Edited by Kurt Winrich

Philip Melanchthon (1497–1560) was Martin Luther's colleague and fellow Reformer. His accomplishments are numerous, but perhaps his most theologically substantial achievement was the writing of the first Protestant systematic theology, the *Loci Communes Theologici*. To accomplish his ordering of theological topics, Melanchthon used the ancient method of the loci, or ordering of topics. In this little treatise, Melanchthon explains his rationale for using the loci method as well as some of his particular ways of using the method.

Philosophers have found it useful to organize the things of this life into categories. Initially they dealt with the things of nature, such as life and death, and then with the form of things. Soon the range was even wider, classifying things as far afield as fate, influence, brilliance, birthdays, and honors. Later, they distinguished those things over which we humans have some power to control, such as virtues and vices. The benefit of all this organization is that the study of these topics has a framework within which to operate, assuring both breadth and depth in our thinking and application. That is, such organization helps prevent us from veering off into irrelevant sidebars. It keeps us focused on the things that are rightly treated in a particular subject. For example, in theology there would be—at least—faith, ceremony, and sin. In the study of law, the topics would include equity, services, crime and punishment, a judge, an advocate, and the like.

So with that background, here's my contention: if you propose to study or understand a topic of human affairs rightly, you should, with diligence and discipline, conduct your study using an appropriate and robust framework. Similarly, if your task is to properly judge others' studies of such things, you would also need to correctly number these topics. And if that's not enough, I'll add that the use of suitable categories is of great help when memorizing.

I hope you now see why I think that scholarly—dare I say intelligent—discussion and study of all things of this life ought to be ordered according to common topics, like virtues and vices and other common themes and common forms. And I'll repeat: this should most definitely be the case for scholarly study.

I also think that this method—a thoughtfully organized framework—ought to be used generally (i.e., outside the academy) for any subject that can be understood by topics. This would include any debate regarding consequential ideas, such as fate, riches, honor, life, death, virtue, prudence, justice, liberality, or temperance. And I'm not leaving out some of the opposing concepts, like poverty, disgrace, exile, the harshness of injustice, disgrace, or the excesses that come from luxury.

I am not alone in these thoughts. Rudolph Agricola has a very nicely composed letter on this idea, as does Erasmus in his *Copia*, where he eloquently expresses his opinion on its use.[1] In fact,

Erasmus suggests that the growth of this "framework methodology"—known among these scholars as the method of the *loci communes*—will be furthered if we read as much as is possible before preparing to organize topics. In his work, he takes a topic, such as vices and virtues, part by part. He then separates the topic into its subtopics. That's only natural, since, as I've already implied, such subtopics are already in the things themselves. For example, the principle of mortality is within the topic of life and death. Erasmus then distributes these subtopics within the overall framework according to their relationship with one another or their resistance to one another.

There are some rules we should follow when using the method of the *loci communes*. One rule would be to understand those topics that are kindred and those that are in opposition. As an example, let's start with what I believe to be the foundational topic of human life, which is piety and impiety. These two should be understood as appearing to be kindred types, though distinct. The first subcategory within piety is love of God, the second is love of country (patriotism), and the third is love of parents to their children (and also children to their parents, which requires them to honor their parents and also teachers). As a quick side note, I remind you that with this type of piety we are all served.

Under the category of impiety, we would place superstition, which in turn includes a very broad array of monstrous worship of other gods (just look at the diverse ceremonies of various heathen peoples). Other subdivisions under impiety would include the invoking of (misplaced) faith in friends, in enemies, and other treacherous persons.

As another example, consider the topic of kindness. To my way of thinking, within the topic of kindness, one must include gratitude. Further, gratitude is found not only in the topic of kindness; it's also found in its opposite. Even more, gratitude is a subtopic of faithfulness. It is certainly present in other topics as well and is important in all of them. Within the topics of virtue and vice, though, the "correct" ranking of all the subtopics is not as clear, so philosophers assign levels of importance as they will.

As you teach the method of the *loci communes*, my best advice is that you should examine the nature and the strength of each argument. I will also suggest—though I know I am biased— that the very most of our enthusiasm and judgment ought to be joined together in the noble study of theology (because it strives toward discerning what is virtue from what is vice) and in the study of civil law (i.e., what is justice, what is equity [ακριβοδικαιον],[2] and what is indulgence [επιεικες][3]). And yes, we should also enthusiastically study every single topic bearing fruit in the description of knowledge.

As you study these topics, I have two strong suggestions. First, I urge you to carefully distinguish fables from real history. This discernment has particular bearing on definitions. As you might expect, in every topic there will be certain important definitions. For example, with the topic of justice, they include what justice is, to whom it is applied, to whom it belongs, and to whom it should be returned.

A word of warning: Although you will see this attention to definitions with other authors who use the method of the *loci communes*, it is sometimes done at the expense of distinguishing fables from real history. For example, just such a lack of discernment can be found in the writings of Gellius,[4] in the writings of Chrysippus,[5] and even more egregiously in the writings of Hesiod[6] (where his teachings concerning justice and good conduct are framed with a fable, from which we get the phrase "And there is virgin Justice, the daughter of Zeus").[7]

So again, I urge you to set aside the accounts of fables or mythology. And not just those ignorantly and arbitrarily concocted but also those narratives that come down from any so-called illustrious author like Hesiod, cited above. Despite his fame and renown, the Hesiodan description of justice based on Plato's *Laws* (*De Legibus*) is one of the worst in this respect.[8]

Returning to the example of justice, I note that wrath is the companion of justice. Justice, of course, is life's great defender but also the nemesis of any who are rash and arrogant (it fulfills these roles with both restraint and precision). Justice is best remembered when the poet declares its fame at any time, anywhere, through beautiful poetry. In fact, if one wishes to praise justice, he should make use of the way Orpheus sang, "He is overlooked and forgotten."[9]

My second strong suggestion is to carefully discern what is opinion. Thus you establish in what way an author is dividing what he knows to be true from what is his opinion. And if you don't know already, you will soon learn that everyone has his own opinion—hence the axiom "let them reveal it in order to maintain their honor."

Theognis[10] the poet was such a man. He embraced the power of justice for everyone, so long as it was lawfully applied, as it is in the use of the morality of Aristotle. There is also the example of Camillus,[11] the conqueror from Falisci.[12] And consider the tale from Cicero's *Brutus*,[13] of Aquilius Manius,[14] who fought on behalf of the empire.

With these examples, one may construct a fluent style of readiness to sort out whatsoever argument he may come across into a sort of *loci communes* of the type as we have received from Cicero's argument for clemency and the restitution of Marcellus in his *Orations*.[15] Thus we ought to assert and proclaim, "Whatever cannot not be said elegantly, is not worth saying." Such was Archias,[16] who was praiseworthy in the cause of humanity.

These are enough examples of the method of the *loci communes*. You should truly not think they are fashioned rashly or randomly. Rather, they are intimate friends, born of the topics themselves, taken out of their very essence. Further, the examples I've cited here provide a brief index of some topics from the last fifteen hundred years. I recommend all those who wish to be enriched by the loci method study them earnestly.

The Uses of the Divine Law

By Philip Melanchthon
(from the 1535 *Loci Communes*),
Translated by Scott L. Keith, PhD

Before we begin, it is imperative to remind the reader that the law of God requires the perfect obedience of the human nature. Further, because the human nature cannot perform this perfect obedience, it follows that men are not pronounced righteous before God on account of the law—our nature always clings to sin. Therefore, the apostle Paul speaks against justification by the law in our corrupted nature.[1] We briefly point this out before delving into the uses of the divine law so as not to infer that the law justifies us. In fact, afterward, these passages will be treated in their entirety.

The Offices [or Functions] of the Law

What are the functions of the law in this corrupted nature? They are three in number.

The First Office of the Law

The first is the civil office—namely, that all men are restrained and contained by a certain discipline. Of this office, Paul speaks in 1 Timothy 1:9: "Understanding this, that the law is not laid down for the just but for the lawless and disobedient, for the ungodly and sinners, for the unholy and profane, for those who strike their fathers and mothers, for murderers."

To establish and accomplish this discipline, God has ordained: (1) magistrates, (2) the law, (3) common instruction, (4) punishments, and (5) human suffering.[2] Also pertinent are sayings of Paul from Galatians 3:24: "So then, the law was our guardian[3] until Christ came, in order that we might be justified by faith."

Thus this discipline, which Paul calls the pedagogy in Christ, is to be praised—certainly because this institution serves to habituate us to what is good, but also because this discipline imposes a certain orderliness on society that in turn enables us to hear and discern the gospel. This wonderful praise [of the civil office of the law] ought to stimulate the intellect of the moderate so that this discipline is not refused. Yet, as I have said above, do not succumb to the opinion that such discipline can merit the forgiveness of sins.

The Second Office of the Law

The second office—the chief office—of the divine law is this: it shows us our sin, accuses us, petrifies us, and condemns the conscience. The apostle Paul speaks frequently of this function, such as when he says in Romans 3:20, "Since through the law comes knowledge of sin." Or when he says in Romans 4:15, "For the law brings wrath, but where there is no law there is no transgression." And in 1 Corinthians 15:56, "The sting of death is sin, and the power of sin is the law." This understanding similarly teaches that the law terrifies the conscience, because it always accuses us. And not only does it make accusations against us; it exposes our natural weaknesses and condemns us for our ignorance toward God, our contempt of God, and our similar mistaken affections.

Thus it almost goes without saying that those who fervently attempt to appease the wrath of God apart from the knowledge of His gracious mercy make no progress but instead are more and more driven to doubt and despair. We can see this in the example of Saul, who, though he sought to be saved by the sacrifices of good works apart from faith, nevertheless could not rest but remained in doubt and despair.

On the other hand, we do not have the law apart from this function—that is, the final mortal blow to men, as Paul says in Romans 7:9.[4] Thus "I was once alive apart from the law"—that is, I was a hypocrite and unworried. But afterwards I perceived my weakness and my sin, and I was terrified. This was how the law was used on King David in 2 Samuel 12:13, when he was reproved by the prophet Nathan on account of his adultery and was petrified.[5]

In short, "contrition," which is called in such cases "repentance," can be clearly understood if we know that these kinds of terrors are real. In other words, these terrors—which are the end of all men—strike out against us not only so we see that we will perish but also so we know we need the kindness and mercy of Christ toward us. As Paul says in Romans 11:32, "For God has consigned all to disobedience, that He may have mercy on all."

This knowledge, then, is a great consolation: when we conclude that we are under sin, the law accuses us not so that we perish but so that we seek the mercy of God. And to be clear that such a great consolation belongs to us personally, the universal saying is added, so all may conclude that His mercy is indeed for all.

The Third Office of the Law

The third office of the law in those who are justified by faith is that which teaches them about good works, about what works are pleasing to God, and about certain commandments in which obedience to God is exercised. For though we are free from the law as far as justification is concerned, the law remains with regard to obedience. But now that we are justified, we are bound to obey God; and indeed, we will begin to do at least some part of the law. And it pleases Him that this obedience is begun in us, since we are pleasing to God on account of Christ.

Conclusion

What is given here appears to be sufficient regarding the uses, or offices, of the law. Now, regarding justification, it must be said again that it belongs to the second use of the law. And again I say the third use belongs in the topic of our works—of the abrogation of the law.

Concerning the Gospel

By Philip Melanchthon
(from the 1535 *Loci Communes*),
Translated by Scott L. Keith, PhD[1]

The term "gospel" is extant in the oldest Greek authors. In Homer, the word signifies one who collects a reward by proclaiming happy news.[2] In Aristophanes and Isocrates,[3] this word signifies a reward given because of something that was done well or because of a report of happy events. The apostle [Paul] himself uses this beneficial announcement.

But the term gospel came to mean a new kind of proclamation so that the law and the new doctrine [gospel] are distinguished in such a way that the new doctrine gains primary influence.

Law and Gospel Are Distinguished

Indeed, this distinguishing between the law and the gospel is the primary consideration. I will not hide behind long explanations or grand arguments but rather provide the necessary distinctions. To wit, it is necessary to distinguish between

- the commandments and the forgiveness of sins,
- the moral precepts and the promises, and also between
- those that are free promises and those that are not free.

Now, as was noted previously, it is the law that demands perfect obedience to God. The law does not remit sins freely, and the law does not pronounce one righteous (i.e., acceptable to God) unless the law is itself satisfied. Sure, the law contains promises; however, it requires the condition that the law be fulfilled (see "not free" above).

On the contrary, even though the gospel speaks of repentance and good works, the benefits that are given are contained in the promise of Christ. This—the promise of Christ—is the fundamental and proper doctrine of the gospel. That's because in Christ the satisfaction of the law for the remission of sins is given freely. Further, the gospel declares us righteous, even though we do not satisfy the law.

Law and Gospel Should Not Be Confused

But how are law and gospel harmonized? The short answer: the gospel is equally preached with the law and repentance, and yet the promise of grace should be expounded in the right way. Let me elaborate.

As most of you know, the law also has promises. Yet the distinction of the promises should be observed. That is, promises are of two kinds in the Holy Scriptures. The first kind pertains to the law and has the conditions of the law. Said another way, they are put forward—promised—on the condition of fulfilling the law. Thus the promises of the law are conditional.

For example, the law teaches that God is good and merciful, but this goodness and mercy is extended only to those who are without sin. By the way, this is the same thing that human reason teaches, which means that through reason itself one can have a certain knowledge of the law. Here, then, everyone can consult himself, for the natural man will find within himself a certain judgment concerning God—namely, that He is merciful, yet only to those who are worthy (i.e., to those who are without sin). The natural man will also conclude—if he's honest—that he can never please God, seeing that he is unclean and unworthy. Thus the law and its promises—whether discerned through Scripture or through reason—leave the conscience in doubt because the promises are conditional.

The second kind of promise is of the gospel proper. Such promises do not have as a cause the condition of the law. That is, they are promised not on account of the fulfillment of the law but freely on account of Christ.

In particular, this is the promise of which the gospel most clearly speaks: the remission of sins [and imputed righteousness] (also referred to as reconciliation or justification). For with the gospel these benefits are certain and not dependent upon the condition of fulfilling the law. If we understand [believe] this, then finally we actually have the remission of sins. But when satisfaction of the law was required, remission of sins was given up as hopeless.

All this means that remission of sins and reconciliation (i.e., justification) is a free gift and is not on account of our dignity or self-righteousness. And yet it was necessary for justice that there be some victim [propitiation] for us. Therefore, Christ was given for us, and He became this victim so that on account of Him we become pleasing to the Father.

Freely on Account of Christ

So in the gospel, we have the promise of reconciliation. This promise is distinctly legal (forensic) because the promise is [given] "freely, on account of Christ." The apostle Paul explicitly uses this particle "freely."[4] Hence we diligently and carefully emphasize "freely." See, for example, Romans 4:16: "Therefore freely by faith, so that the promise is sure."[5]

Now, this particle, "freely on account of Christ," is what distinguishes law and gospel. If we do not notice this particle of the free promise, doubt will remain in our minds, the gospel will be transformed into law, and nothing will communicate to our consciences the remission of sins or justification. If we do not notice this particle of the free promise, then all we have is our natural judgment (our reason), which is the law, not gospel.

Therefore, our adversaries, even if they cry that they are teaching the gospel, still leave the conscience in doubt because they do not teach that reconciliation is free, and in place of the gospel they teach the law, as in Hesiod[6] (i.e., the judgment of natural reason).

Thus this particle, in our eyes and minds, is to be understood as emphasizing "freely." To this end, it is necessary that we teach that this is a gracious promise. Our objective is threefold: that the promise is certain, that the conscience is set free from doubt, and that we have firm consolation from true terrors. For in these things it is truly realized that this work is a gracious promise. Most of all, though, it is our contention that this is the chief doctrine to which all others are referred.

Yet it ought to be noted: the promise should be received. Paul teaches this in Romans 4:16: "Therefore freely by faith so that the promise is sure." And 1 John 5:10 says, "Whoever does not believe God has made him a liar" and so on. Accordingly, the term "freely" does not exclude faith but removes the condition of our dignity [self-righteousness] and transfers the cause to our benefit in Christ. Neither is our obedience excluded, yet the total cause of the benefit is transferred from our obedience to Christ so that the benefit is certain. Therefore, even though the gospel preaches repentance so that the reconciliation is certain, we teach that the remission of sins and God's pleasure do not come to us on account of the dignity [righteousness] or the "newness" of our repentance. This is necessary for the consolation of faithful consciences. And hence it is easily judged how these things agree, that we can teach the gospel of repentance and still preach the free promise of reconciliation. But I will say more about this comparison a little bit later.

Christ, in the Gospel of Luke, gives the ultimate definition of the gospel clearly as a verbal artist, when He describes it in chapter 24, verse 47: "And that repentance and forgiveness of sins should be proclaimed in His name to all nations, beginning from Jerusalem." This is the preaching of the gospel repentance and promise, which reason does not naturally grasp, but God reveals it when He promises that He remits our sins on account of Christ, and we are pronounced righteous after receiving the Holy Spirit and eternal life as a gift. This He promises freely, so that it is certain.

Let this then be the definition of the gospel, in which three components are embraced as the proper benefits of the gospel—namely, that

1. our sins are freely forgiven for the sake of Christ,
2. we are graciously pronounced righteous [on account of Christ], and
3. we are reconciled and are received as heirs of eternal life [on account of Christ].

These three components we will explain a little later. Here, it is only necessary to remember the proper benefit of the gospel, which can otherwise be summed up in one word: justification.

Justification and Faith

By Philip Melanchthon
(from the 1535 *Loci Communes*),
Translated by Scott L. Keith, PhD,
Edited by Kurt Winrich

As I have said previously, the gospel is the highest teaching of repentance and remission of sins on account of Christ. Therefore, concerning justification, I say predominantly this: the gospel wars with sin and teaches that we need Christ to be our mediator, for it is on account of Christ we are granted remission of sins and reconciliation.

If such is the case, it follows unavoidably: one cannot speak of justification without also speaking of remission of sins. Sadly, there are some (buffoons, I say!) who, with many words, have explained justification, all while making no mention of the remission of sins—as if it had no bearing on the matter! And yet these same people believe that God moves the hearts of infants and sanctifies them when they are brought to Him in baptism!

But we digress. Here we are speaking of adults, who, according to the teaching of the gospel, are those who must believe in accordance with the express will of God. That is, their terrified minds must rest in the knowledge that sins are forgiven freely, through mercy and grace, on account of Christ. And they must similarly know that this free forgiveness is not given on account of the dignity, sincerity, or strength of their contrition, or their love, or any other of their works. In this way, God changes our minds by faith and gives reconciliation and the forgiveness of sins.

If this is not the case—and the judgment finally is that it is sufficient that we have remission of sins as a result of our contrition or our love—our minds would be driven to despair, never knowing if we have enough contrition or love. Therefore, that we may have a sure and firm consolation, free remission of sins does not depend on us at all but solely on the mercy and grace promised, on account of Christ.

These concepts would be nothing absurd, difficult, or complicated if the Scriptures were regularly and sufficiently engaged in the churches. If so, it would be well known that attributing any merit to our works serves only to make the remission of sins uncertain. Even better, the people of our churches would be comforted in the fact that remission of sins is a gift—not dependent on our works—and therefore is completely certain.

So in that spirit of engagement, let us look more deeply at the word "justification," which we contend points to the cause. We say justification signifies remission of sins and reconciliation (or acceptance) of the person to eternal life. Is this what the Scriptures mean?

To start, note that for the Jews of Jesus's time, justification was a forensic word, "forensic" meaning having to do with judgments in courts of law. So if I said, "Scipio has been justified from the accusations of the tribunals and the Roman people," that would indicate that he has been pronounced righteous or absolved.[1] Therefore, when Paul uses the words "to be justified," we take these to mean, according to the first-century Jewish understanding, reconciliation and the remission of sins (i.e., absolution). Furthermore, when God remits sins, He simultaneously gives the Holy

Spirit, who creates new virtues in the faithful. So we freely believe, teach and confess—and with a clear voice—that it is not only faith that should exist in the faithful but also more fruit of the Spirit. But that's another topic, of which we shall speak later. For now, it seems clear that this forensic understanding of justification means remission of sins is ours neither because of our decision nor because of our dignity or merit. Rather, it is a gracious pronouncement, apprehended through faith.

Doubtless, for Paul, faith—as this "cause" of justification—signifies trust in promised mercy on account of Christ. Even while some (cheaters and fools, I say!) thoroughly and loudly protest and deny that faith means to trust in mercy and grace, I doubt, however, that any of them appeal to learned and virtuous men for this opinion. Jan van Campen, a wise man (even though he sometimes criticizes us in this discussion), rather prudently sees this. That is, in Paul, [faith] must be understood as this same confidence in mercy.[2] This demonstrates that my interpretation is fair. Of course we do not exclude the knowledge of the history of Christ and His saving person and work, as some falsely accuse us of doing. For when we say confidence in mercy promised on account of Christ, I certainly embrace all the articles of faith, and we certainly also refer to that article that is the history of Christ, which brings to mind the benefits of Christ—that is, the forgiveness of sins. Therefore, this [faith] includes both trust and knowledge of Christ the Son of God, as well as action (or habit) of the will, by which it receives the promise of Christ, and thus, acquiesces in Christ. This sets aside fancy rhetoric. This faith, therefore, signifies trust in the mercy of God, which by example bears witness.[3]

So we speak here of faith in the context of justification. And we reiterate that this is from the teachings of Paul. Paul conveys the promise of grace and faith, and we take hold of this promise through faith. Furthermore, this faith is trust in the mercy of God. Trust, in this whole debate, looks down on our merit and requires confidence in a righteousness not of ourselves—an alien righteousness—namely, the righteousness of Christ. Now, if Paul thought that man was righteous (i.e., acceptable to God or reconciled) on account of his dignity, qualities, or works, he would have taught that he had confidence in his own merit. On the contrary, it is known that he says in Romans 3:27, "Then what becomes of our boasting? It is excluded." Again, he calls us to Psalm 32:1: "Blessed is the one whose transgression is forgiven, whose sin is covered." And so, we are immediately pronounced righteous when we believe that our sins are forgiven. Now this faith, which confesses that sins are remitted, is the trust of which we speak. Also with what is said in Romans 5:1: "Therefore, since we have been justified by faith, we have peace with God through our Lord Jesus Christ." For this is contrasted with the knowledge of the law, of which it is said in Romans 4:15, "For the law brings wrath, but where there is no law there is no transgression."

Although the arguments from works are common and natural, faith is contrasted in that it always signifies trust in the mercy of God, promised on account of Christ. We certainly believe in this article as the remission of sins. Furthermore, the "common and natural" opinion is reprehensible, because it delivers nothing but doubt about whether we have remission of sins. Faith, therefore, is intimately connected to God's mercy; indeed, God's mercy is the object of faith. This is why it is said that we are justified by faith. So that the figure of speech may be rightly understood, let me say it this way: justification is by the mercy of God promised on account of Christ, but this mercy is grabbed hold of by faith. I encourage you to read again Romans chapter 3, where Paul says that man is reconciled not on account of the dignity or qualities of their works but by trust in an alien righteousness.

Notes

The Method of the "Loci Communes"—1526

1 See Desiderius Erasmus, *On Copia of Words and Ideas (De Utraque Verborum Ac Rerum Copia)*, trans. Donald B. King and Herbert David Rix (Milwaukee: Marquette University Press, 1963).
2 *Summum jus* (Greek, ἀκριβοδίκαιον) is the origin of the maxim "*Summum jus summa injuria* is lost in antiquity." It is that overly perfect kind of justice that has obtained, by its merits, the title of the opposite vice.
3 Justice beyond ordinary justice.
4 Aulus Gellius was a Latin author and grammarian.
5 Chrysippus of Soli was a Greek Stoic philosopher.
6 Hesiod is one of the earliest Greek poets, often called the father of Greek didactic poetry.
7 See Hesiod, *Works and Days, Theogony, and the Shield of Heracles*, trans. Hugh G. Evelyn-White (Mineola: Dover, 2006), ll. 248–64.

8 See Plato, *Laws*, trans. Benjamin Jowett (Champaign, IL: Project Gutenberg, 1990).
9 See Pseudo-Hyginus, *De Astronomica*, 2. 7.
10 A tragic poet spoken of contemptuously by Aristophanes.
11 Camillius, Marcus Furius, was the savior and second founder of Rome.
12 The Faliscans were the inhabitants of the lower Ager Faliscus near Mt. Soracte.
13 Cicero's *Brutus* (also known as *De claris oratibus*) is a history of Roman oratory. See Graham Vincent Sumner, *The Orators in Cicero's Brutus: Prosopography and Chronology* (Toronto: University of Toronto Press, 1973).
14 Probably a son of Manius Aquillius, a consul in 129 BC; he was a loyal follower of Gaius Marius. During the election campaign for Marius's fourth consulship, Aquillius was left in command of the army in case the migrating Cimbri attacked before Marius could return to command the army himself.
15 See M. Tullius Cicero, "For Marcellus," in *The Orations of Marcus Tullius Cicero*, trans. C. D. Yonge (London: George Bell & Sons, 1891).
16 He was born in Antioch in Syria (modern Antakya in Turkey) and was known as an *improvisatore* orator. In 62 BC, he was accused by a certain Grattius of having assumed the citizenship illegally, and Cicero successfully defended him in his speech "Pro Archia."

The Uses of the Divine Law

1 E.g., Rom. 3:20, Gal. 2:16, Gal. 3:11.
2 Here Melanchthon uses *"calamitates humanas"* (human calamity or suffering), saying that such is encompassed in the first office of the Law. He is using this in the same sense as Paul in Rom. 5:1–5 (ESV): "Therefore, since we have been justified through faith, we have peace with God through our Lord Jesus Christ, through whom we have gained access by faith into this grace in which we now stand. And we rejoice in the hope of the glory of God. Not only so, but we also rejoice in our sufferings, because we know that suffering produces perseverance; perseverance, character; and character, hope. And hope does not disappoint us, because God has poured out his love into our hearts by the Holy Spirit, whom He has given us."
3 παιδαγωγὸς, or *paidagōgós* (from *país*, "a child under development by strict instruction")—properly, a legally appointed overseer authorized to train (bring) up a child by administering discipline, chastisement, and instruction (i.e., doing what was necessary to promote development).
4 Rom. 7:9 (ESV): "I was once alive apart from the law, but when the commandment came, sin came alive and I died."
5 2 Sam. 12:13 (ESV): "David said to Nathan, 'I have sinned against the Lord.' And Nathan said to David, 'The Lord also has put away your sin; you shall not die.'"

Concerning the Gospel

1 Special thanks to Mr. Kurt Winrich for editing this piece and making it clean and readable.

2 *The Odyssey*, bk. 14, l. 152: "εὐαγγέλιον δέ μοι ἔστω"— that is, "And let me have a reward for bearing good tidings." Homer, *The Odyssey*, ed. G. P. Goold, trans. A. T. Murray, 2 vol. in the Loeb Classical Library [No. 104] (Cambridge, MA: Harvard University Press, 1919–98). See also *A Greek-English Lexicon*, 9th ed., with a revised supplement, ed. H. G. Liddell and Robert Scott (Oxford: Clarendon Press, 1996). "εὐαγγέλιον: the reward of good tidings, given to the messenger; in the Christian sense, the Glad Tidings."

3 εὐαγγέλνα θυειν, or "sacrifice for good tidings." *Theological Dictionary of the New Testament*, ed. Gerhard Kittel, trans. Geoffery W. Bromily, vol. 2 (Grand Rapids: Eerdmans, 1964), 723. "In religious usage, the message is again so highly valued that it is equated with the actuality. On the occasion of these messages sacrifice is offered not merely for the message (εὐαγγέλνα θυειν) but for the event proclaimed. εὐαγγέλνα is thus estimated as a fact in the oracles of the imperial cult."

4 *Particula Exclusiva*, or "exclusive particles." This indicates the radical exclusion of works from salvation by grace and the radical exclusion of merit by the gracious application of Christ's merit to believers (e.g., grace without works).

5 "So the promise is received by faith. It is given as a free gift. And we are all certain to receive it, whether or not we live according to the Law of Moses if we have faith

like Abraham's. For Abraham is the father of all who believe" (Rom. 4:16).

6 *The Oxford Classical Dictionary*, eds. M. Cary et al. (Oxford: Clarendon, 1949), 423. "Hesiod—Ἡσίοδος—son of an unsuccessful citizen of Cyme in Aeolis, who with his two sons, Hesiod and Perses, migrated to Greece and settled at Ascra on the slopes of Helicon. Sometime after the father's death Perses, who had already obtained more than his share of the estate, tried, with the help of the rulers, to obtain still more. It is not known how the dispute was settled, but it appears to have lead Hesiod to begin a series of moral admonitions in hexameter verse which afterward resulted in the poem 'Works and Days.' Herodotus makes him a contemporary of Homer, but later antiquity is uncertain. The modern opinion generally regards him as later than Homer, but there is no agreement on the date."

Justification and Faith

1 *The Oxford Classical Dictionary*, eds. M. Cary et al. (Oxford: Clarendon, 1949), 815. "Scipio Africanus Major, Publius Cornelius (236–184 B.C.), son of Publius. In 199 Scipio was elected censor and became *princepes senatus*. A keen supporter of a philhellinic policy, he prudently but vainly urged in his second consulship (194) that Greece should not be completely evacuated lest Antiochus of Syria should invade it. In 193 he was sent to Carthage to investigate a frontier dispute between Carthage and Masinissa. When his

brother Lucius was given command against Antiochus (190), Africanus, who could not constitutionally yet be reelected consul, was 'associated' with the command. After crossing to Asia, where he received back from Antiochus his captured son Lucius, Scipio fell ill and took no active part in his brother's victory at Magnesia (189). Meanwhile in Rome, political attacks, led by Cato, were launched on Scipios, culminating in the 'Trials of the Scipios,' on which the ancient evidence is conflicting. Africanus intervened when Lucius was accused in 187; whether he himself was formally accused either in 187 or 184 is doubtful. But his influence was undermined and he withdrew embittered and ill to Liternum where he died soon afterwards (184)." See also W. Schur, *Scipio Africanus und die Begründung der römischen Weltherrschaft* (1927); H. H. Scullard, *Scipio Africanus in the Second Punic War* (1930).

2 Melanchthon uses the Latinized version of his name, "Campensis." See Peter G. Bietenholz and Thomas Brian Deutscher, *Contemporaries of Erasmus: A Biographical Register of the Renaissance and Reformation*, 3 vols., The Collected Works of Erasmus, vol. 1 (Toronto: University of Toronto Press, 1995), 255. "Jan van Campen (Campensis), who was descended from a respected family from Kampen, in Overijssel, completed his education in the University of Louvian, where he may have been preparing for a theological degree and the priesthood as early as 1509. The independent and scholarly bent of his mind led him to focus on the study of the Bible and of Hebrew. He had shown interest in the early works of Luther and Melanchthon, but it does not seem that even

the Louvain theologians found any reason to question his orthodoxy."

3   For Melanchthon, "saving faith" (*fides salvifica* or *fides propria*) is a true personal faith made of three parts: (1) *notitia*, or knowledge of the historical Christ and His saving person and work; (2) *assensus*, assent to the intellectual truth of that knowledge; and (3) *fiducia*, or trust—that is, a faithful confidence that, by an act of the changed will, appropriates savingly the mercy of God shown on those who trust in Him on account of Christ. Saving faith cannot, therefore, be merely historical or intellectual—it is volitional.

www.ingramcontent.com/pod-product-compliance
Lightning Source LLC
Chambersburg PA
CBHW062035120526
44592CB00036B/2141